anythink

D0753270

WHAT'S BENEATH

PEEKING UNDER
YOUR SKIN

by Karen Latchana Kenney

illustrated by Steven Wood

PICTURE WINDOW BOOKS
a capstone imprint

It is a hot summer day. Sweat rolls down your face. Your skin feels wet. Take a deep breath and fill your lungs with air.

Your body is a wonderful machine. Many systems work together so you can breathe, eat, and play. But these systems are hidden. Your skin covers and protects them.

Want to see what your
body parts look like?
Lift the page to peek beneath...

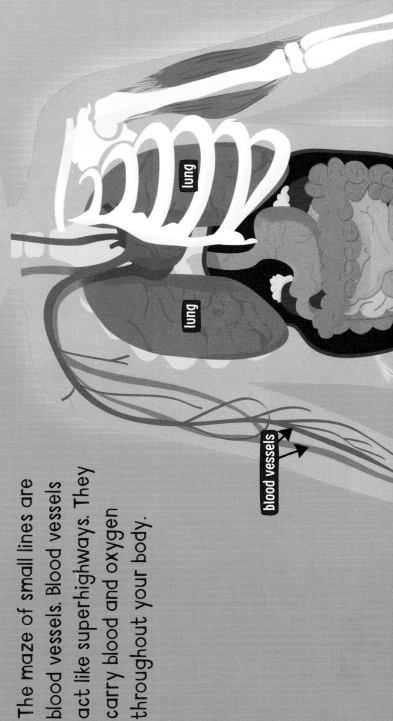

lung

lung

blood vessels

Your skin is just one thin layer of your body. Many body systems and parts lie beneath it. Each one has a special job.

The maze of small lines are blood vessels. Blood vessels act like superhighways. They carry blood and oxygen throughout your body.

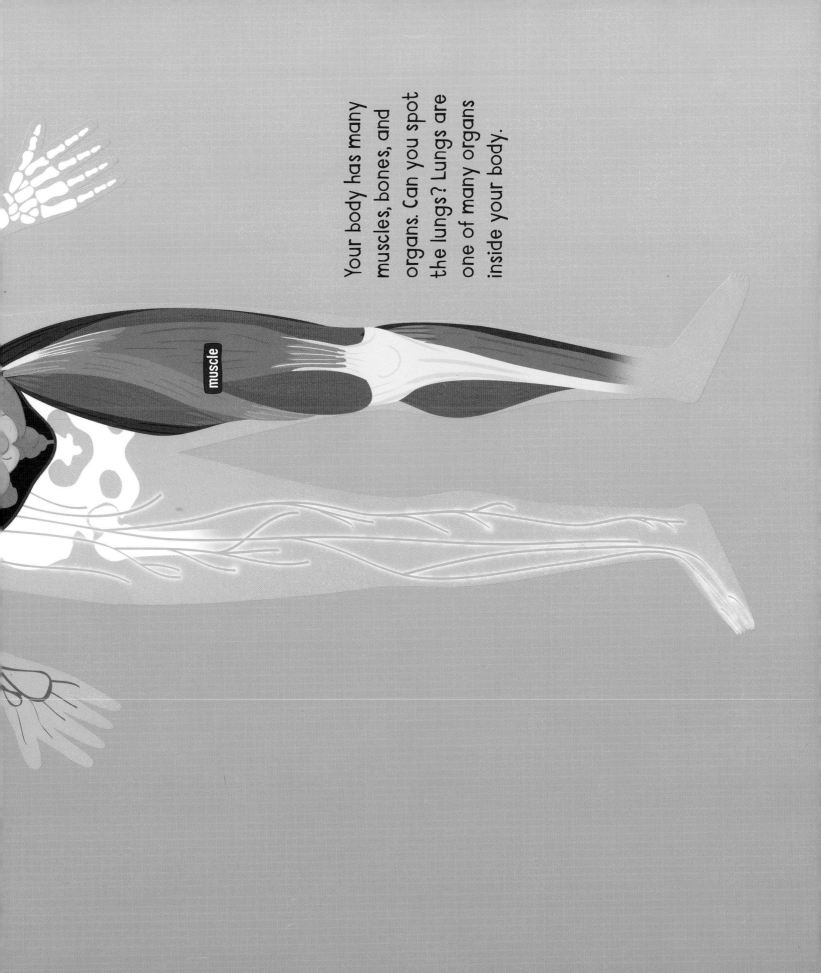

Your body has many muscles, bones, and organs. Can you spot the lungs? Lungs are one of many organs inside your body.

muscle

Cover Up!

Let's start at the surface. The skin is a bumpy place. There are dips, pockets, and hairs. The top layer is the epidermis. It sheds dead skin cells all the time.

Just below the epidermis is the thickest skin layer. It's called the dermis. See its fibers? They keep the skin strong. They also hold water. Many small blood vessels keep skin warm.

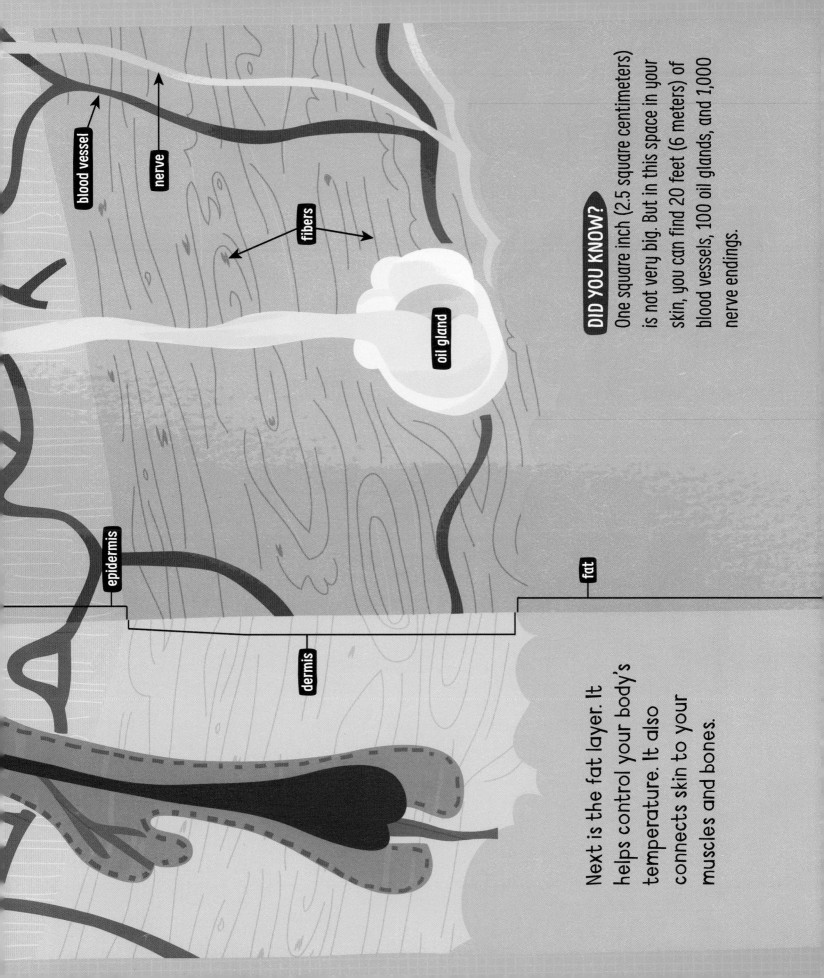

blood vessel

nerve

fibers

oil gland

epidermis

dermis

fat

DID YOU KNOW?
One square inch (2.5 square centimeters) is not very big. But in this space in your skin, you can find 20 feet (6 meters) of blood vessels, 100 oil glands, and 1,000 nerve endings.

Next is the fat layer. It helps control your body's temperature. It also connects skin to your muscles and bones.

Keeping Cool

If your body gets too hot, it won't work well. Sweat helps keep you cool.

Sweat comes from sweat glands. It is made mostly of water and salt. Sweat holds body heat. It travels through tiny tubes. Some tubes go directly to the skin's surface. Other tubes connect to hair follicles.

hair

hair follicle

sweat

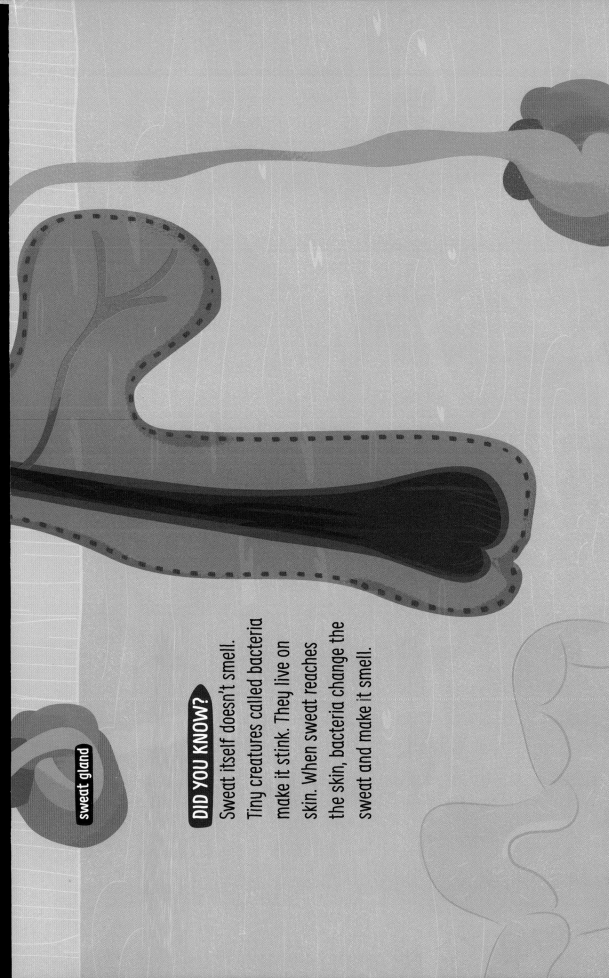

sweat gland

DID YOU KNOW?

Sweat itself doesn't smell. Tiny creatures called bacteria make it stink. They live on skin. When sweat reaches the skin, bacteria change the sweat and make it smell.

When sweat dries, it takes heat away from the body. This process is like natural air-conditioning.

Hello, Hair

Skin is covered in hair. The skin on top of your head usually has the most. Just below your scalp are close to 100,000 hair follicles. The follicles work nonstop to push hair through the skin. A single strand of hair begins at the hair root.

See the blood vessels? They feed the root's cells. The cells make a protein. The protein becomes the hair shaft. The hair grows longer and moves up the follicle.

hair shaft

gland

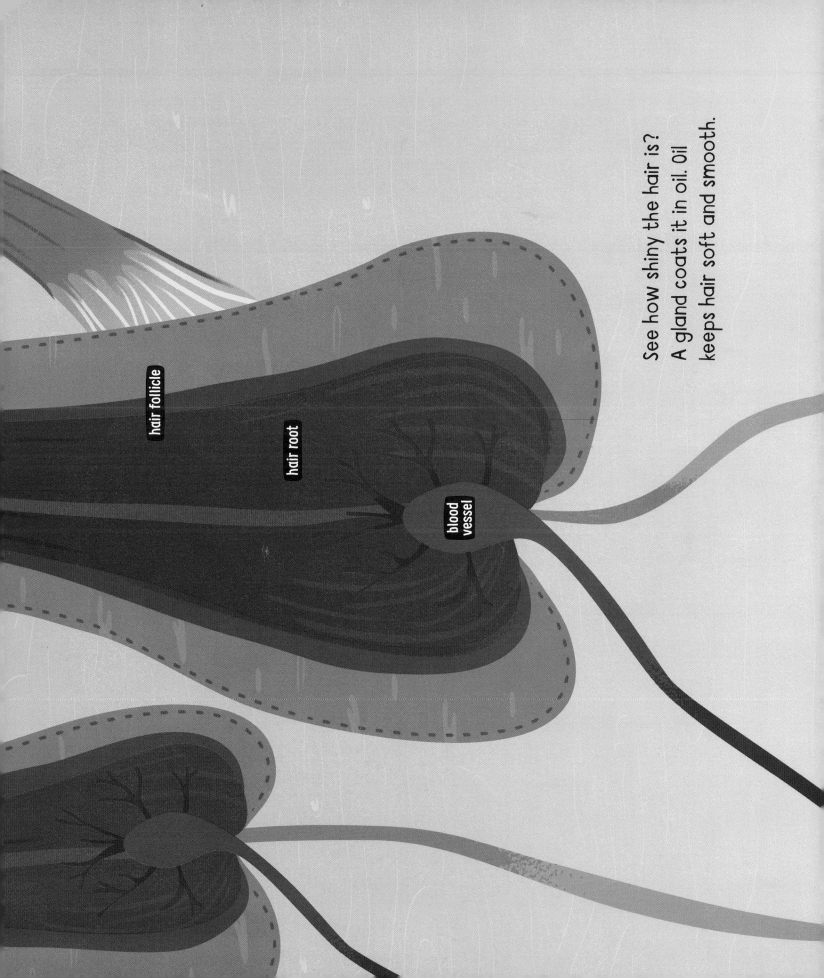

hair follicle

hair root

blood vessel

See how shiny the hair is? A gland coats it in oil. Oil keeps hair soft and smooth.

Superhighways

Your hair needs blood to grow. So does every other part of your body. Blood is made up of cells and plasma. It carries oxygen and nutrients throughout your body. Blood also takes away waste.

How does the blood move? Along "highways" of blood vessels. These highways are super long. If placed in one line, your blood vessels would stretch 60,000 miles (96,560 kilometers)!

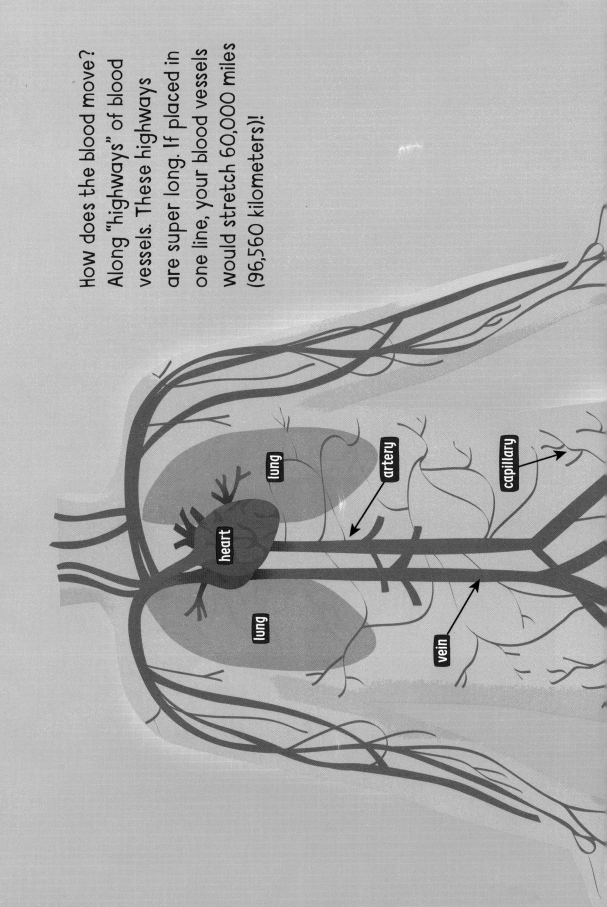

lung

lung

heart

artery

vein

capillary

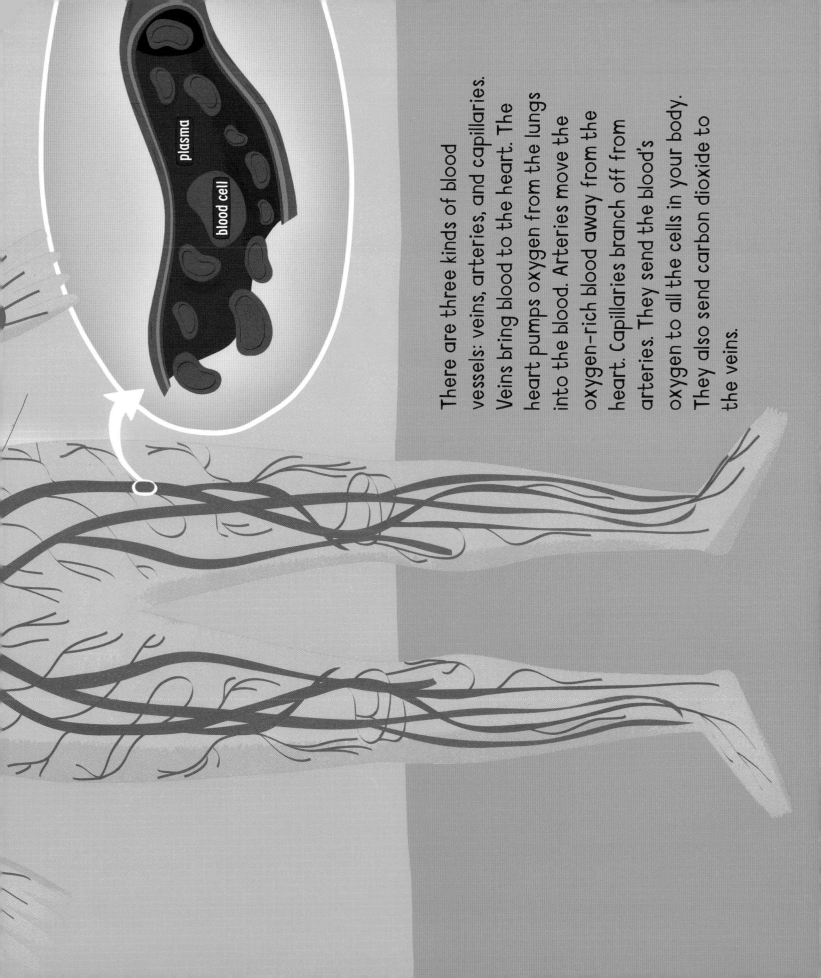

plasma

blood cell

There are three kinds of blood vessels: veins, arteries, and capillaries. Veins bring blood to the heart. The heart pumps oxygen from the lungs into the blood. Arteries move the oxygen-rich blood away from the heart. Capillaries branch off from arteries. They send the blood's oxygen to all the cells in your body. They also send carbon dioxide to the veins.

Breathing Machine

Oxygen needs to get into your body to feed the blood. When you breathe in, air enters your nose or mouth. See where the air goes? It moves down the trachea.

See where the trachea splits? Those tubes are the bronchi. They lead to the lungs. The tubes get smaller and smaller. They become bronchioles.

nose

mouth

oxygen

carbon dioxide

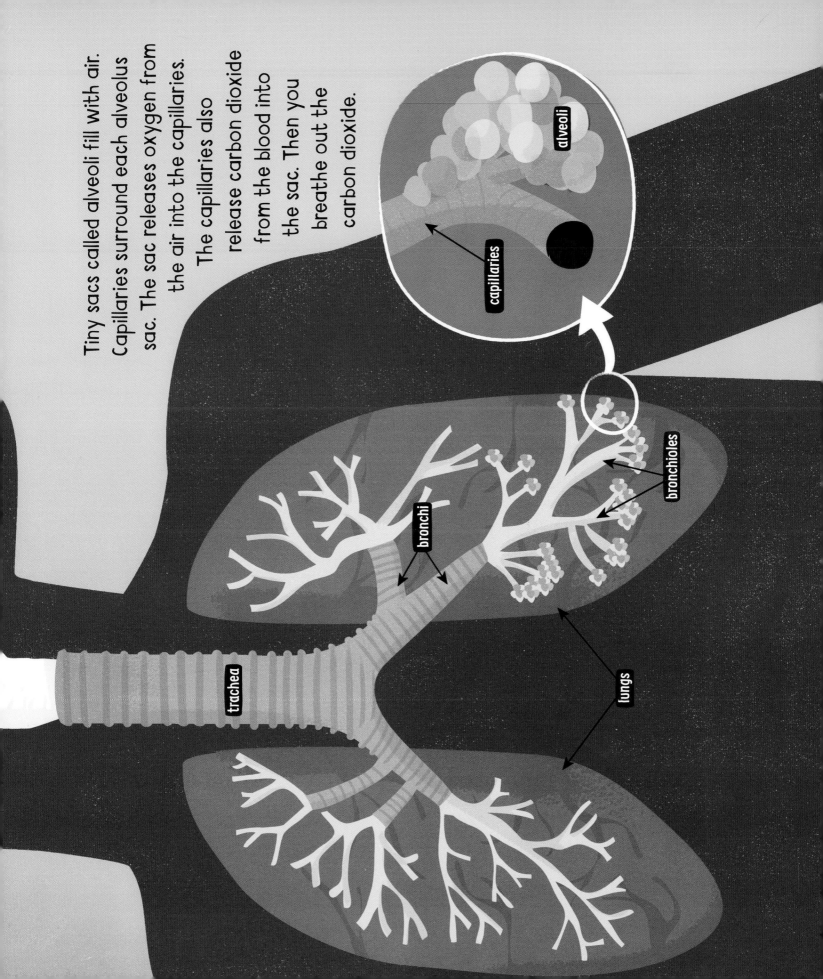

Tiny sacs called alveoli fill with air. Capillaries surround each alveolus sac. The sac releases oxygen from the air into the capillaries. The capillaries also release carbon dioxide from the blood into the sac. Then you breathe out the carbon dioxide.

alveoli

capillaries

bronchioles

bronchi

trachea

lungs

Pumping Blood

To move oxygen-rich blood throughout the body, you need a good pump. And you have one: your heart! This hardworking organ beats 100,000 times each day. It powers the body's circulatory system.

See how the heart has two sides? Each side sends out blood through the pulmonary artery. The blood travels to the lungs to pick up oxygen. From there it zips back to the heart through pulmonary veins. The oxygen-rich blood goes out to the body through the aorta. Each side of the heart has two chambers.

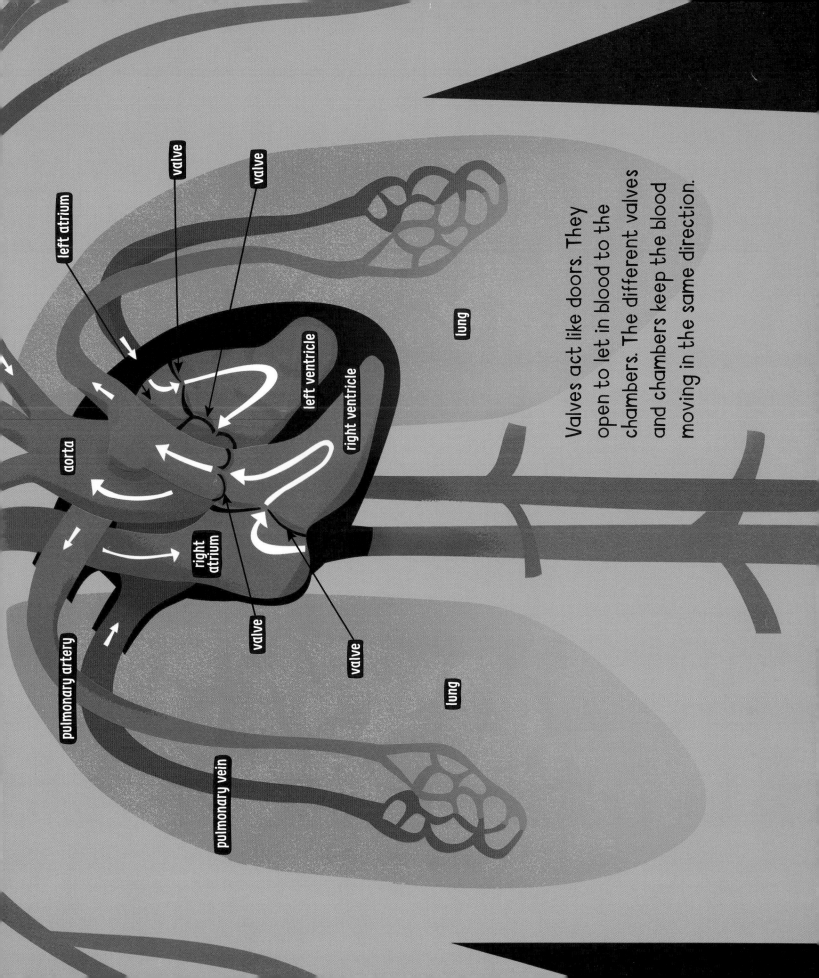

left atrium

valve

valve

left ventricle

right ventricle

aorta

right atrium

valve

valve

pulmonary artery

pulmonary vein

lung

lung

Valves act like doors. They open to let in blood to the chambers. The different valves and chambers keep the blood moving in the same direction.

The Fuel Factory

The body needs blood and oxygen to work well. It also needs fuel to power its systems. This fuel comes from food. Food gets broken down in the body's digestive system.

Let's follow a bite of apple. When you take a bite, your teeth break down the apple. Then the apple bits move down the esophagus. Plop! They land in the stomach. A mixture of acids and enzymes in the stomach further breaks down the apple bits.

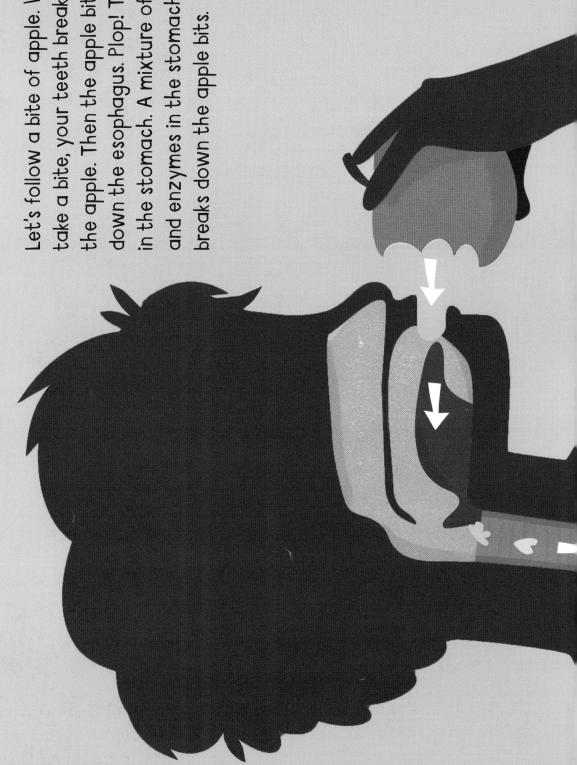

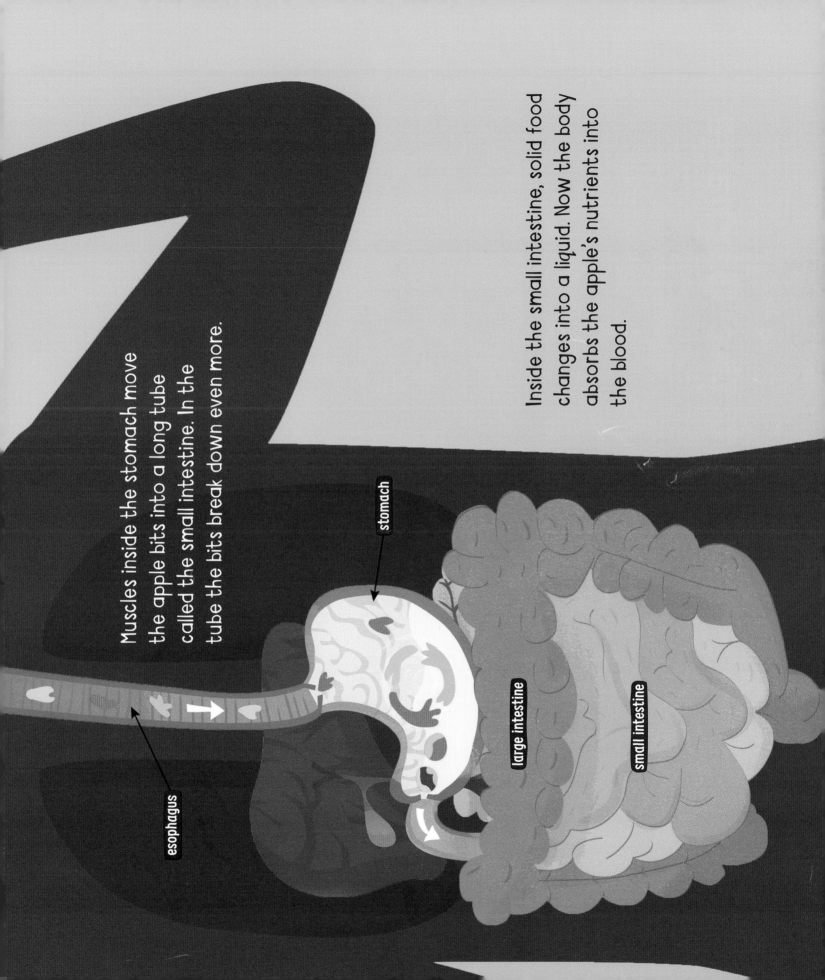

Muscles inside the stomach move the apple bits into a long tube called the small intestine. In the tube the bits break down even more.

Inside the small intestine, solid food changes into a liquid. Now the body absorbs the apple's nutrients into the blood.

esophagus

stomach

large intestine

small intestine

Take Out the Garbage

Not all parts of food become fuel. The body has to get rid of liquids and solids. They leave the body as waste. The large intestine takes out solid waste.

It moves in waves. The waves push waste to the rectum. Waste collects there until it leaves the body through the anus.

large intestine

anus

rectum

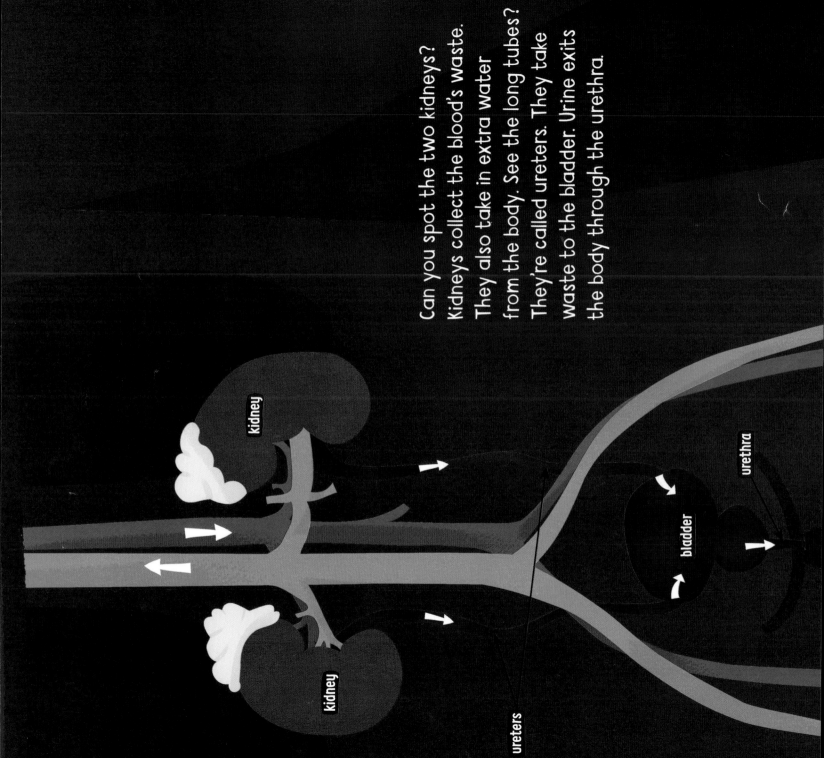

Can you spot the two kidneys?
Kidneys collect the blood's waste.
They also take in extra water
from the body. See the long tubes?
They're called ureters. They take
waste to the bladder. Urine exits
the body through the urethra.

kidney

kidney

ureters

bladder

urethra

Get the Message?

You can sense when you have to go to the bathroom. Your body sends your brain a message. Pain is another type of message. All messages travel through the body's nervous system. They travel faster than the blink of an eye.

Let's say you get stung by a bee. First the pain message moves through nerve fibers in the skin. The fibers connect to the spinal cord. Different nerve cells there receive and pass on the message. The nerve cells send the message to the brain.

The message reaches the thalamus. The thalamus knows which part of the brain needs the message. Parts of the brain control different movements and areas of the body. Your brain thinks of how to stop the stinging pain. It then sends a message back through the nervous system. It says, "Move your arm away from the bee!"

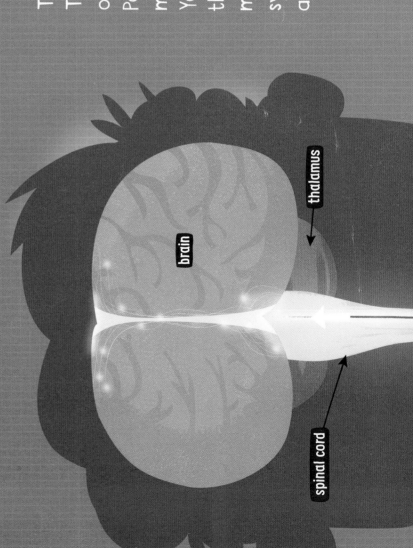

brain

thalamus

spinal cord

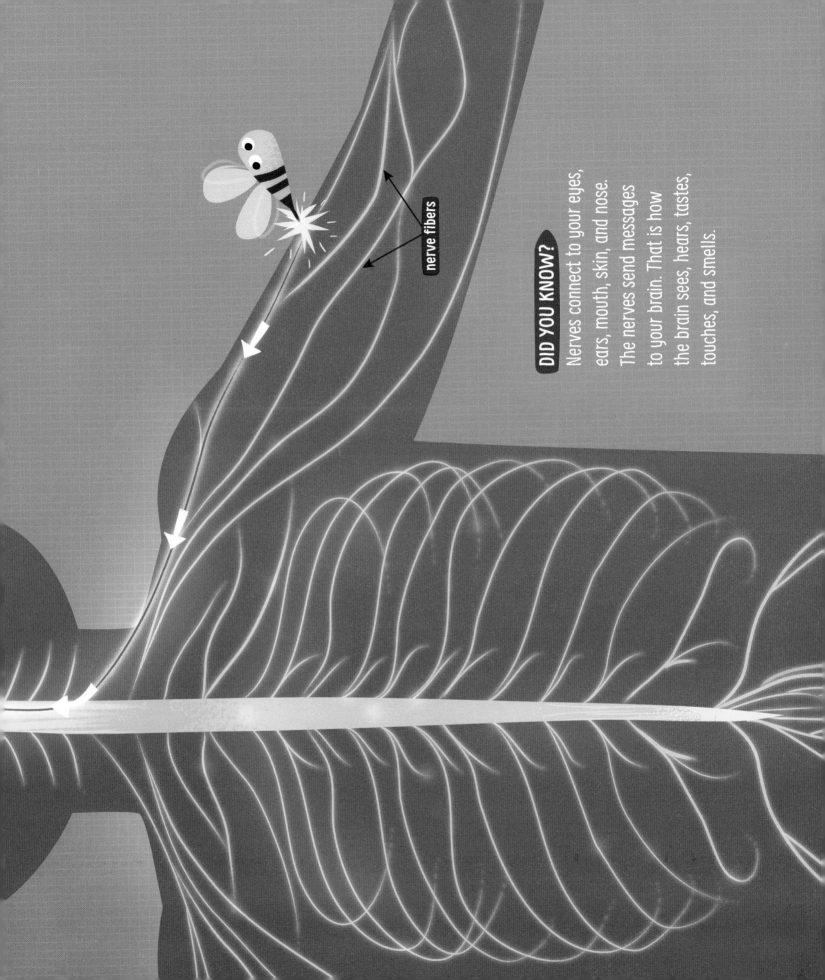

nerve fibers

DID YOU KNOW?
Nerves connect to your eyes, ears, mouth, skin, and nose. The nerves send messages to your brain. That is how the brain sees, hears, tastes, touches, and smells.

Taking Control

Certain parts of the body need chemicals to work. These chemicals are the body's hormones.

See the different glands? They are hormone factories. They take materials from blood to make hormones. Then they release the hormones into the blood.

Look at the hypothalamus in the brain. Its hormones help you sleep and wake up. Hormones from the thyroid gland control how your body uses food. The thymus gland helps you fight off illness.

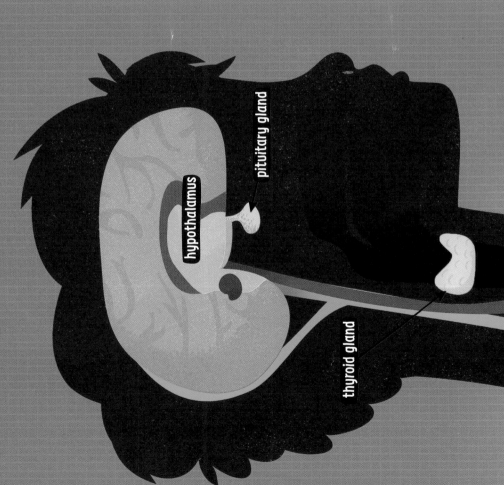

hypothalamus

pituitary gland

thyroid gland

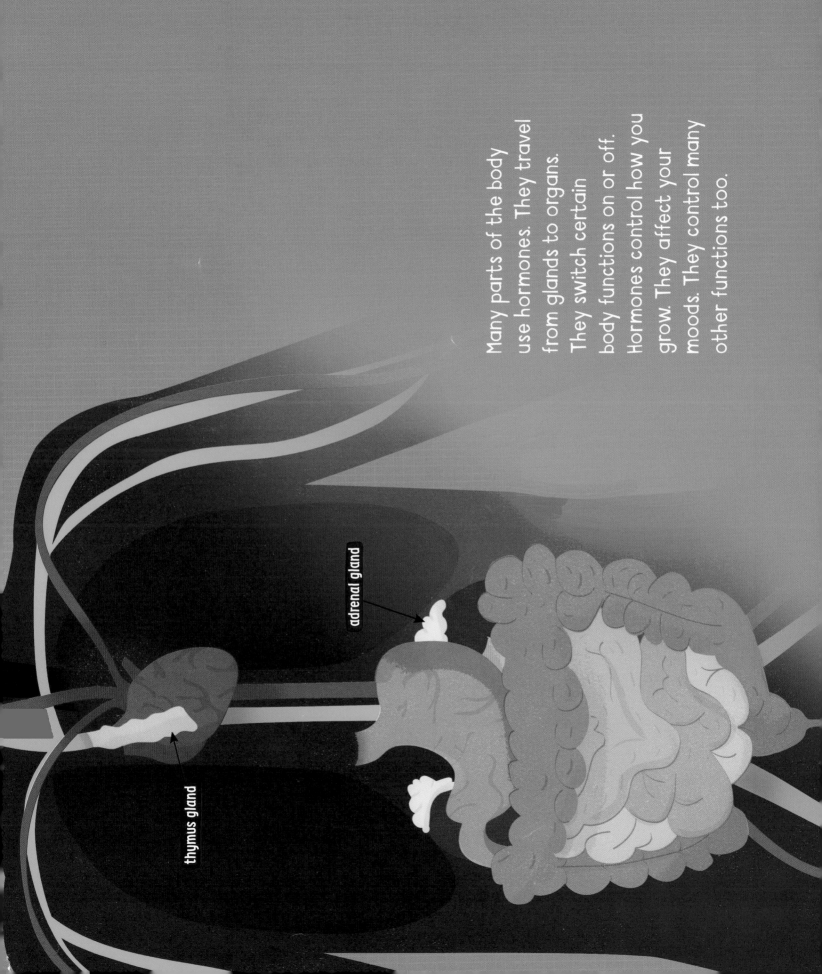

Many parts of the body use hormones. They travel from glands to organs. They switch certain body functions on or off. Hormones control how you grow. They affect your moods. They control many other functions too.

adrenal gland

thymus gland

Bones and Muscles

Hormones control how your skeleton grows. Your skeleton is your body's frame. It is made of the bones inside your body—more than 200! It holds you upright. It also protects organs inside the body. See where the bones come together and connect? Those spots are called joints.

Many muscles cover your skeleton. See the tendon? It connects to the bone. Nerves send messages to muscles, telling them to move. The muscles stretch or shorten. Bones move with them.

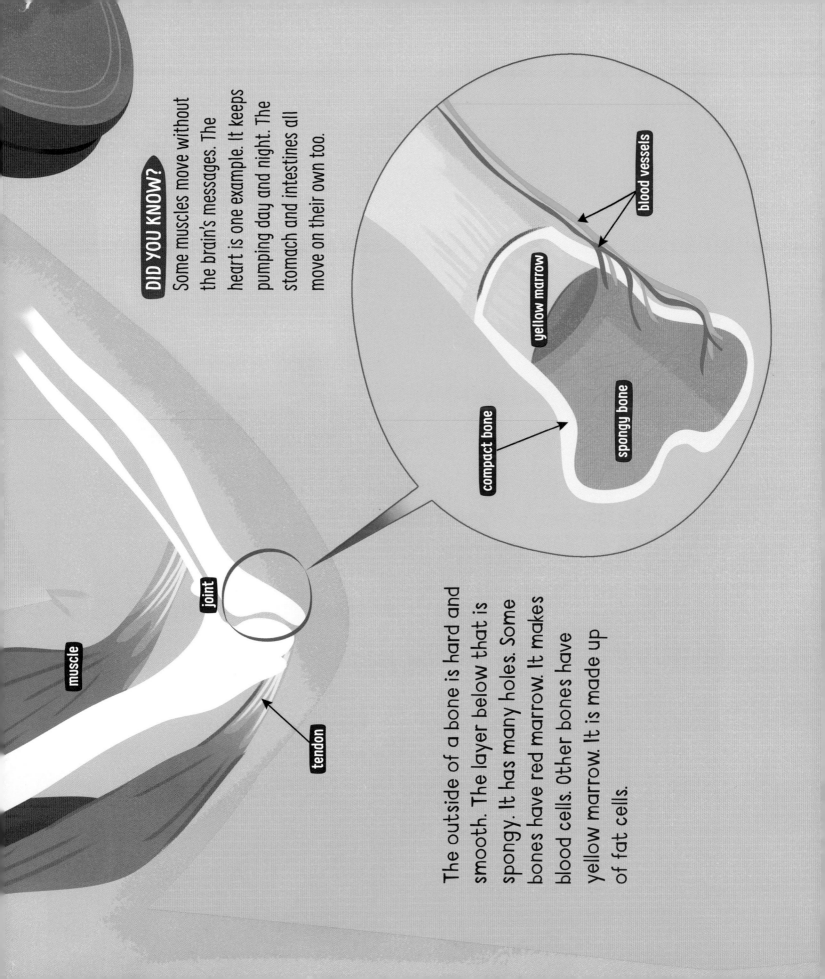

Some muscles move without the brain's messages. The heart is one example. It keeps pumping day and night. The stomach and intestines all move on their own too.

muscle

joint

tendon

blood vessels

yellow marrow

compact bone

spongy bone

The outside of a bone is hard and smooth. The layer below that is spongy. It has many holes. Some bones have red marrow. It makes blood cells. Other bones have yellow marrow. It is made up of fat cells.

Wipe the sweat from your skin. Find some shade. Time for a cold glass of lemonade! The human body is an amazing machine from the outside. And now you know how amazing it is inside too!

GLOSSARY

absorb—to soak up a liquid

acid—a liquid that can break down different materials, such as food

artery—a tube that carries blood from the heart to parts of the body

bacteria—tiny living things that live on or around your body; some are helpful and some are harmful

carbon dioxide—a gas that people and animals breathe out

fiber—a long and thin thread of a material, such as a muscle

gland—a body organ that makes chemicals

muscle—a body part connected to bone that makes you move

nutrient—a protein, mineral, or vitamin that makes you strong and healthy

organ—a body part that performs a certain job, such as the heart

oxygen—a gas found in air that people breathe in and use in their bodies

plasma—the liquid part of the blood

urine—a body's liquid waste

valve—a moving part that controls how a liquid or gas flows

vein—a tube that carries blood back to the heart

CRITICAL THINKING USING THE COMMON CORE

1. What do the kidneys do? (Key Ideas and Details)

2. Look at the illustration of the lungs. Use it to explain what happens when you breathe in and out. (Integration of Knowledge and Ideas)

3. Describe how a sandwich gets from your mouth to your small intestine. (Key Ideas and Details)

READ MORE

Canavan, Thomas. *How Your Body Works*. Mineola, N.Y.: Dover Publications, 2015.

Holland, Simon. *Human Body: Can You Tell the Facts from the Fibs?* Mankato, Minn.: Picture Window Books, 2016.

Kolpin, Molly. *Why Do I Sneeze?* Mankato, Minn.: Capstone Press, 2015.

INTERNET SITES

FactHound offers a safe, fun way to find Internet sites related to this book. All of the sites on FactHound have been researched by our staff.

Here's all you do:

Visit www.facthound.com

Type in this code: 9781479586684

Special thanks to our adviser, Marjorie Hogan, MD, Department of Pediatrics, Hennepin County (MN) Medical Center, for her expertise.

Picture Window Books are published by Capstone,
1710 Roe Crest Drive, North Mankato, Minnesota 56003
www.mycapstone.com

Editor: Jill Kalz
Designer: Russell Griesmer
Creative Director: Nathan Gassman
Production Specialist: Katy LaVigne
The illustrations in this book were created digitally.

Printed and bound in US
007536CGS16

Library of Congress Cataloging-in-Publication Data
Cataloging-in-publication information is on file with the Library of Congress.
ISBN 978-1-4795-8668-4 (library binding)
ISBN 978-1-4795-8672-1 (paperback)
ISBN 978-1-4795-8676-9 (eBook PDF)

LOOK FOR ALL THE BOOKS IN THE SERIES:

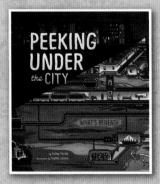
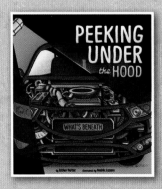
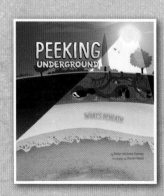